This book is to encourage women to get out of their
abusive relationships and make a better life for themselves
and their children.

This is my truth and God has blessed me to tell my story, in
order to bless others.

"RUN LADIES and DON'T LOOK BACK"

RUN

Let Go of the Abusive Relationship and Run Into Your New Future

© 2019 by La'Shunda Gardner
runnowladies@gmail.com

Published by Sow The Seed Ministries
296 Jared Tyler Rd
Glasgow, KY 42141
Printed in the United States of America

TABLE OF CONTENTS

INTRODUCTION

I am not a psychologist or a counselor. This is my life experience, and I want to share it with you, to encourage you. My story may be different than yours, but we all have a story. My goal is to express to you that you are valuable. You are an angel. You are worth it. You are more than a conquer. Regardless of the mistakes you have made, you are forgiven. It is up to you to start now and begin a new life for yourself. I cannot make you change your life. You have to do it yourself.

Are you ready? It is time. "Let's go and enjoy life. Let's make new goals. Let's try new things." Let's start over. In order to do that, you have to RUN! Are you ready? Let's take the first step. It is up to you. When you get sick and tired of being sick and tired, I hope you step out and RUN! The only way you can get to point B is to step out of point A. It sounds easy, but sometimes we sit in our mess or comfort zone and waddle in it.

Let's do this ladies, let's RUN!!

THE BEGINNING

Everything is always good in the beginning. This is the impressive stage. You must impress him to get his attention. You both lock eyes and the first date happens. You are so excited. Everything goes well, you enjoy his company. You cannot live without him. He is all you think about, daily. Your day is filled with joy because you have found your Prince Charming.

You see, I was there once. I was happy to be in a relationship, in my early 20's. He was an older guy. I enrolled into college, stayed on campus, and believed I was ready to live my life as an adult. Just a reminder, just because you turn 18, does not mean your mind is mature enough to handle every adult situation.

We started dating and we were all smiles. As a matter of fact, we could not stop smiling. We were so shocked that we were actually dating. I was his girlfriend and he was my boyfriend.

We discussed our dreams and goals. We talked about having kids. Since he was older, he tried to school me about relationships. For example, he mentioned that the man was the head of the household. This is true, but his head of the household was totally different than God's. He wanted a woman that cooked, cleaned, and took care of the household. That sounded good in the beginning, but did not end the same way. I was new to having a "REAL" relationship, so I listened. I was head over heels for this guy. I listened and believed anything he said. You see, I wanted this relationship to work, so it was pretty easy to persuade me.

HE WILL CHANGE

This relationship lasted six years, three of which we were married. We moved in together and things were exciting. It was new, so you make each day happy. He set some ground rules that he did not abide by. One was to keep our family business in our house. He did not practice this. I later found out he told a lot of our relationship business to his family. They could tell me things that we experienced, during our marriage. I had no idea they even knew about these situations. At the time, I was fine with keeping our family business to ourselves. Though I did not know he was not participating. Remember, I was 20 years old and I was fine with anything this guy said. Everything was great, or so I thought.

At the age of 21, I had our daughter. We were so happy. We had our family, our own house, this was the life. Well at least I thought it was. I stayed home with our daughter, the first year, before going to work. I made sure the home was taken care of, food was cooked, clothes were ironed, and everything else that would please my man.

At the time, I did not realize it, but this was exactly what he wanted. His main lady at home, and others outside of the home. I was the main. I was the one he took around his family and friends to make it seem as if his married life was so lovely.

The women started or should I say, they never ended. They were there before me and continued after me. When you are in love, you tend to not see things the way they are. The way he looks at other women, the comments he makes about them, and the way he acts around certain women, to name a few. But I looked over it, because I just knew he would change.

I WILL NEVER LET A MAN HIT ME

I had always said, even before I started dating, "I would never let a man hit me." I would hear people talking about men and women fighting in their relationships. So I was determined to not let that happen to me. Now this relationship was about control. He wanted to be in control of everything and everybody. With me being home the first year, he knew where I was at all times. I just did not know exactly where he was and what he was doing. We had one car, so I had no way to go any place, and that is the way he wanted it.

It started with the arguments. He liked to argue. I saw it in the beginning, but of course, I figured he would change. He liked to dominate our conversations and arguments. I could never get a word in, and he was always right. His voice was so loud it could be heard outside. He did not care. He wanted to get his point across and did not care about mine. He started to transform the pretty, well dressed girl that he once loved, into the baggy clothes wearing girl, that he started to hate. He did not like me wearing clothes that were fitted. He liked them loose, so men would not look at me. The women he stared at all wore tight fitted clothes and he enjoyed the scenery.

When we would argue his face would look so evil, as if he wanted to punch me. He would put his finger so close to my face, without touching it, hoping I would smack it out of the way. He wanted a reason to hit me. That would give him an excuse to say, "Well she hit me first." So I never did, because that is what he wanted me to do.

I can remember a time we got into a heated argument and he pushed me. I thought, "No he didn't. This dude just pushed me." And of course when things calmed down, he apologized and I just figured this is what happens in a relationship. So now my thoughts of him changing turned into "I will change him."

HE SAID HE WAS SORRY

The relationship continued to go downhill, but we acted as if it was doing well. Or should I say, I acted this way. I later found out every time I left, everyone, like his family and friends, knew about it. Each time I left, I went to my mom's house. The arguing started to be every other day. It became normal. If there was a two-day period without an argument, I knew something was wrong.

I would hear things that he was doing and bring them to him. Of course he would deny them. I had someone tell me that they saw him out with a female. He would go out with his friends, and come home with red lipstick on his shirt collar. He would accidentally lose track of time, and forget to come home at a decent hour. But I would let things slide and move on like they never happened. But things just did not make sense. The screaming kept coming and I started screaming back. I was not a screamer but I soon became one. He would always take things that I accused him of doing and flip them to make it seem like it was me. He was a good manipulator. He was the type that you could see doing something but he swore that it was not him. And then he would always say he was sorry and how much he loved me. I wanted to believe him. I wanted a happy family.

I AM GETTING TIRED

The arguing was an everyday thing now. I was always being accused of cheating, although he was always the one running the streets and in the studio late nights into the morning…Really? I started hearing and seeing more evidence that it was time to go, but I was scared. I was scared of him, and I was scared of being on my own raising a toddler.

I had to realized that it did not matter what I did, how much I tried to please him, he never thought I was special enough to care about me, the way GOD wants a husband to care about his wife. I kept seeing more and more confirmation that he was cheating. I even was able to hear my confirmation, because I saw his passcode that he used, to check his voicemail for his pager. Each time his pager beeped, and he did not call back, I took note of the time, and remembered his facial expression, and excuse for not returning the call. I would later go and listen to all of his messages. I started keeping a log showing the name, time, and the reason for her call.

I remember there was an outdoor show, in Atlanta. He was so happy to go with his friends. I asked to go and of course he said I could not. Well from the looks of it, that was not my cup of tea anyway. What caught my attention was he wanted to go shopping and buy things that did not fit this outdoor show. The items were more for a romantic occasion. I was much older now and becoming wiser. I knew a woman had to be involved. Of course I was able to listen to his voicemail and verified I was correct. This time it was different. I was building up some guts and getting bold. When he came home from his trip, I was acting happy to see him and asking about his trip. I even had the house smelling good and cozy. I told him to push play on the boom box and turn on the music. Well it was not Teddy, that he heard, but it was a female from his voicemail. He was pissed. Oh was he pissed, he was extremely pissed. You see I had gone behind his back, got his personal passcode, and listened to his voicemail from another female. He ended up making up a dumb story and made it seem as if it was my fault. I was the one in the wrong.

I was getting tired. I was tired of being faithful and getting nothing in return. I needed a way out, but I was still scared. I had left twice. I started saying to myself, "My dad does not raise his voice at me, so why would I let this guy do it?", "I can do bad all by myself", and "Marriage has to be better than this."

THE KICK

I was fed up, but this was a different fed up. You see there was another argument, but it was worse. The screaming was louder to where one of my neighbors told me that she could hear the arguments in the middle of the night. She asked if I was okay. Of course I said, I was fine. But in the back of my mind, I knew this was coming to an end.

We argued on this particular day and I can remember finding myself on the floor and my jaw was shaking. Why was it shaking? He kicked me in the face. Yes, you read it correctly. He kicked me in my face. He picked his nasty barefoot up off of the floor and kicked me in my face. I went to pick up the phone to call '911' but this big and bad guy knocked the phone out of my hand. Now if he was really bad he would not have stopped me from calling the police.

You see I started out saying, "I will never let a man hit me." What I should have said was "I will never let a man treat me less than who GOD created me to be, his wife." You think I left after the kick? No, I was shocked that it happened. I knew I needed to leave, but I still did not leave. And of course he said he would change. But all I heard was "blah, blah, blah."

THE LAST STRAW

After the kick, although I stayed and acted like I was fine, I started thinking of a strategy plan to leave. It was time. My thoughts about him had changed for good. This guy does not love me. He does not care about me. Sometimes I think he hates me. He accuses me of everything when I am doing nothing, but going to work, school, and taking care of our household.

I am a spiritual person and I knew it was time, when I started thinking about things that were not normal to me. Things I knew were not pleasing to GOD. I started thinking of ways to kill him. Now this was about 2001, so I do not have these same thoughts now. I knew it was time to leave. I cooked, washed, and cleaned, so there were many ways to do this. He always fell asleep everywhere. It would have been pretty easy. But because this was out of my character, I took a different route. A route more pleasing to God. I decided to RUN.

I HAD TO RUN

After calling my mom and telling her what had happened, she said, "You cannot continue to leave and then go back. No one will ever believe you." I later realized that each time I left, he was out celebrating with the ladies. My mom called back and said, "Bring my grandbaby over here right now, and get yourself out of that mess."

I believed God blessed me then, and he is still blessing me now. I was grateful that our daughter was not home the majority of the times to remember the fights and arguments. That is truly a blessing. Sometimes we do not realize how much our children watch and listen to what we do and say. They watch every step we make. This is why we must pay close attention to what we let in our children's minds. We can corrupt their thought pattern at an early age and not realize it.

At the age of four, our daughter did not understand why her daddy was not around all of a sudden. I had to gradually explain to her that, "Mommy and Daddy are not together anymore, and we still love you." She loved her dad and that is another reason why I could not kill him. I wanted our daughter to have both parents. She loved us both.

I started praying to God and he started confirming. I was still wondering if I had made the right decision. The decision of leaving, even after being pushed, kicked in the face, talked to like a dog, and being cheated on. I am just being honest. I thank God for giving me the strength to RUN and the ability to figure the rest out later. I had to delete all of the negative sayings that this man told me and replace them with positive sayings such as, no one will ever love you like I do. You're correct, someone else will love me better. You cannot make it out there on your own. He was correct again, but I am not on my own, God is with me every step I take. You will be back. After the third time leaving, I told him that God would have to stand in front of me and tell me to go back. Well it has been since 2002, and God never showed up for that one. The only difference is this time; I was listening to God.

I did not talk to many people about my relationship. I wanted this relationship to work. I only heard God when I felt I needed him badly. I know you may say, "But you did need him." I know, I just did not want to hear what he had to say. After the kick, I knew it was time to go, and I was not trying to stay long enough for another one.

YOU HAVE TO RUN LADIES

Every day you think things will get better. You try to forget about yesterday like it never happened. You do not think to run, because you know he will change. He was sorry. He did not mean it. But deep inside you are in pain and do not know which way to turn. You feel lost, but show a happy face when around others. He shows a happy face and portrays to be a happy husband.

A lot of women do not make it. **I WANT YOU TO MAKE IT!** In order to do this, you must RUN. Do not look back keep running. Grab a bag, your baby, and RUN. Get out of there. You can do bad all by yourself. Run like your life is on the line, because it is on the line. RUN now and explain later. Your kid will not understand now, but when they are older, they will either forget or remember running with momma and crying. Think about your safety and your children's safety. Love yourself first. Okay, love God and then yourself. No one should talk down to you, make you feel less than, or make you explain every move you made for the entire day. I know you wanted a family. I know you want to be with the father of your child. Is it worth losing your life? Is it worth not seeing your kid attend first grade, their first soccer game, or trips to the playground? Is it worth not being able to see their first monkey bar fall, when they land on their bottom, and you run to hug, kiss, and let them know that everything is okay? Is it worth missing your first rejection of not being able to kiss them on the cheek, because it is now embarrassing, as a six-year-old in front of their friends? Is it worth missing their smile when the tooth fairy comes to visit? Is it worth missing their first _____? You can fill in the blank.

Are you still thinking about running? Why not run? What are you losing? Oh you think you are losing him? Well let me tell you, "He is already gone." If he was there, he would be treating you like a queen. You need to RUN. I had to run. I could not write this book for you, if I did not run. You may have a story that you need to tell, in order to help others. You cannot tell it if you stay.

Maybe he has some insecurities within himself, and he takes it out on you. That is his problem and not yours. He needs to change himself, and you do not need to be there. If God wants to put you back together, he will, but until then…RUN!

YOU STILL NEED TO RUN

Since you are still there let me help you out. Run now and do not look back. You need to run with all the strength you have left. You will need every bit of it. You are at your lowest right now and it is time to escape this mess. If you have to be at a low, be there because of you and not because someone else took you there. Gather the small amount of self-esteem and courage you have left, and run like you are running a marathon. It hurts when you start but you will gain much when you finish. Take a bag, the kids, and run. Do not look back. There is nothing but HELL there. Keep looking and pushing forward. Your new life is coming.

But you can only get there if you RUN.

YOU DID IT

I am so proud of you! You did one of the hardest parts: you left. I know you are nervous and maybe even scared, but you are free. You are free to do what is needed while you are still living. Let me tell you again, "I am so proud of you!!" Give yourself a hug. You are awesome.

Now that you have stepped into a new chapter of your life, let me give you some encouragement. When I left the final time, my emotions were all over the place. I was happy that I left but scared to do new things. I was nervous to move into my new apartment. I wondered what others would say when I saw them, whether it would be, "I told you so," "I am glad you left," or "You should have stayed." People said all of those things, but they did not know about the abuse. So, it was easy to see why some thought we should have worked things out.

I lived with my mom for a while and looked for an apartment. The apartment manager called and stated she did not have any vacancies. I was sad, but I knew God had me covered. He would help me find what I needed. Two weeks passed, and I received another call from the apartment manager. She stated someone had moved unexpectedly, and she would have the apartment cleaned so my daughter and I could move in. I was so excited and nervous at the same time. I was stepping out and taking a leap of faith knowing God was right there with me.

I remember when I was a little kid I heard older women speak about having Peace of Mind at my church, Galilee

Missionary Baptist. I stared and sometimes laughed, especially when I saw them jumping and running around the church giving their praises to God. But when I first moved into my apartment, I understood what Peace of Mind meant. Now I was the one running around my house and screaming praises to God. I can remember seeing my grandmother, Ormigene Washington, singing gospel songs with a smile on her face while cooking Sunday dinner. Seeing her smile made me smile, too. What I could not see was who was following her. Now when I am in my kitchen singing gospel songs and cooking Sunday dinner, even when I am stressed about a situation, I have a smile, too. As I walk, I feel a presence hover above me that moves with me. I take another step, and the presence moves again. I make a turn, and he says, "I got you. You don't have to worry about a thing."

STARTING OVER

As I gathered my items to move, I did not have a lot, but I had what I needed. I did not have a house full of furniture. Two church members came to me one Sunday and said, "I heard you were moving. We are getting new furniture. We have a sofa bed and dinette set that you can have, and we will deliver it to you."

To myself I said, "Thank You, God." I got what I needed, and it was delivered to me. When we take that step of faith, God will send others to help. So now I had a sofa bed that I used as a couch and my bed, a dinette table with four chairs, a day-bed for my daughter, a dresser that my dad gave me, a small radio, and a television (it was not a flat screen).

I tell you this just to let you know I did not have a house filled with things, but my mind was clear and free. I was able to sleep without an argument. I did not have to worry about being questioned about my entire day. I did not have to worry about my spouse coming home late at night with made up excuses about where he had been. I felt the peace. I now knew what Peace of Mind really meant. Regardless of what was going on in the outside world, my mind was clear and without any worries.

DO NOT GIVE UP ON YOURSELF

Life is not over. This is just the beginning of a new chapter of your life. Forgive yourself for any mistakes you made in your relationship and move forward. As I was in my apartment, I started reflecting on my life. What did I want to do? What was next for me? I am free.

Learn yourself again. I lost a part of me in that relationship. I could not even tell you what I liked to do, if you had asked me. If you asked my favorite color, it was probably his favorite color. So now that you have left the relationship, write down your goals. Write the things you want to accomplish before you leave this earth. I do not care if your dreams seem unrealistic to you. Do not look at where you are now, look at your future. When writing your goals, you may not be where you want to be now and that is okay, but you can start taking the necessary steps to get there.

To set your goals, start with eight sheets of paper. On the first page write Now as the title. On the next seven pages write 3 Months, 6 Months, 9 Months, 12 Months, 2 Years, 5 Years, and 10 Years. Write down all of your goals and your dreams. Make sure each goal reflects this acronym S.M.A.R.T: Specific, Measurable, Attainable, Realistic, and Time-Bound. For example, if your goal is to lose weight, using the acronym, you would write, "I want to lose 70 pounds in one year." Break your goal down by dividing 70 pounds by 52 weeks, which is 1.34 pounds per week. This goal is specific, measurable, attainable, realistic, and time-bound. Each week just make sure you stay within your calorie count, get some exercise in, and you should reach your goal. Baby steps are good. If you mess up and, for example, eat too many cookies like I sometimes do, it is totally fine. It may take more time to reach your goal, but you are closer than you were yesterday.

The point is you have a plan. You are making positive changes. This is an accomplishment. If you are trying to lose weight, check with your health insurance company to ask about additional programs and benefits for subscribers. For example, I have Blue Cross Blue Shield of Tennessee and they offer Blue365, which has a lot of discounts and gives discounted rates to local gyms. Just call and find out what your plan offers. I enjoy my plan; I just need to use it! I am still working on my goals, just like you.

If you want to go back to school, do it. There are so many resources available for you. There is probably a scholarship for women that have left a relationship due to domestic violence. You just never know what is available until you start asking for help and researching. If you feel you are not smart enough or you do not remember what you learned in high school, go to the library. Check out a book and read it. We have so much time on our hands, but always say, "We do not have time." Put the cell phone down, turn the television off, and read. Believe me, I am preaching to myself, too. We all have 24 hours in a day. What are you doing with yours? I was blowing mine by doing nothing, and I will never get that time back.

If you decide to further your education, you may want to speak with a representative from your local high school, a technical school, or a community college counselor. You can ask about grants and scholarships during that time. You may check with your local library for additional resources also. Currently with my Nashville Public Library card, I am able to get free access to Lynda.com, which is a subscription-based service that provides thousands of tutorials. I previously paid for a subscription to Lynda.com, and now I can log in with my library account for free. I use this site when I need a refresher or to learn new software. There are so many videos to choose from, so check and see if your state provides this service.

If you decide to start using a budget here is a suggestion. Write down your total take-home amount for the month (net income) and your total amount of out-go for the month. Include all utilities, groceries, fuel for car or bus fare, household items, daycare, and then subtract your out-go from your total take-home. Whatever is leftover will give you an idea of what is remaining whether it is $50, $0, or -$150. If you have a negative balance, look for ways to remove items from your out-go that are not necessities. If you have extra money, put it to the side for an emergency fund. Do not get overwhelmed. The fact that you sat down and made a budget is a good start. This will take longer than 15 minutes, and that is okay. When my husband and I do our monthly budget, it can take close to an hour. And to be honest, I blow it a lot, especially in the grocery category. You can spread this process out to two days. I just want you to get an idea of what you have coming in compared to what is going out.

If you would like a closer relationship with God, I suggest you read Romans 10:9 in the bible. If you want to learn how to pray, start by saying, "Dear God….." you can continue the rest. You can say anything. "I really do not believe in you," "I am scared," "I do not know what to do," or even, "HELP!!!" Whatever you say or ask is okay. He will answer at the right time. When I want to make sure my answer is strictly from him, I ask him to give me a sign. There are times when I pray to God, but then my mind starts to wonder what his answer will be and then I get all confused wondering if he gave me the answer or if I tried to answer my own question. However you wish to start is up to you. Meditation also helps.

I still do not want you to give up on yourself. Do not harm yourself. I know you thought you would be further along in life, married, have a business, or have kids, but you are not there yet. You are not too old. If you woke up this morning, you have another chance to start. DO NOT COMMIT SUICIDE! I need you here to tell your story. When God is ready for you, he will come by and pick you up. He does not need your help. Stay strong and fight through the pain and hard times. Once you make it out, you will be able to look back, feel the accomplishment, and be so proud of yourself. Do not give up on yourself.

There are several resources available for you. Here is a list of a few:

May Parrish Center – 615-256-5959

- Provides help for domestic violence survivors and their children

Metro Action Commission – 615-862-8860

Tennessee Housing Development Agency – 615-815-2200

United Way – 1-800-318-9335

- Offers rent and utility assistance, senior services, counseling services, basic needs, after school programs, and more

National Suicide Prevention Hotline – 1-800-273-8255

If you are feeling suicidal, please reach out to someone for help. I was told as a kid, people that saw a psychiatrist or counselor were "Crazy." That is what I always believed, until now. We all need someone to talk to. We are hearing more about mental illness and others are speaking out; therapy does not seem so bad. Most of the time we call our bestie and rant in their ears, but they do not always tell us what we need to hear, but rather what we want to hear. Professional help is available if needed. You are not crazy, and there is nothing wrong with you if you decide to seek professional help.

BEING ALONE

When you are single you may be lonely sometimes, especially after spending so many years in a relationship. Instead of feeling sad and alone, learn how to love yourself again. Learn how to be happy again. It is okay to be alone. We need the space at times. Give your kids big hugs and tell them how much you love them. Look in the mirror and say to yourself, "I Love You. I am Beautiful. I am Somebody. I am Successful. I can do whatever I set my mind to do."

I had to regain my self-esteem, because I lost it. I had to remind myself how beautiful I was. I knew I was cute when I was younger, but I had to remind myself that I was still cute after my divorce. I am not only cute on the outside, but on the inside, too. We must remind ourselves and know this for ourselves. We do not need to get validation from anyone else.

FORGIVENESS

Forgiveness can be a tough one. Sometimes we say we have forgiven someone, but when we dig way down, the hurt and unforgiveness are still there. I wondered why God advised me to write a book now and not in 2007, five years after the divorce. He took me on a journey and had me look at my life during that time. So, in 2002, I was divorced, had low self-esteem, my faith was not the best, I was not as wise, and I most definitely had not forgiven my ex-husband. So now in 2019, I am remarried, my self-esteem has been regained, my faith is so much stronger, I am much wiser, I have accomplished most of my dreams and goals, and I have forgiven him.

People can only do to us what we allow them to do. Forgive yourself for allowing him to mistreat you. We all make mistakes. Some mistakes are harsher and the consequences may be greater than others, but we all make them. Try to forgive. It is not easy; it took so much of my energy to keep thinking about that relationship. Finally I just decided to let it go and forgive him. It was draining me.

THE NEXT WOMAN

Now that the relationship is over, you may start seeing your ex with other women. It will hurt, and you may want to cry. Stay strong and wait to cry at home. I know it is painful but you both will move on eventually. When this happened to me my only prayer was that his new woman respected our child. I did not want anyone mistreating our daughter. I am so grateful that no one ever did. Nowadays, you just do not know about some people.

God recently revealed something to me. He spoke about my past marriage and that I did what I was supposed to do as a wife, but it still did not work out. He mentioned how I saw and heard that my ex-husband treated his new woman better than he treated me. I can remember asking God years ago, "Why does he take her family places that he never took our family? Why does he treat her better than he treated me?" God did not respond then, but he has now. God said, "He has to treat her better than he treated you. If not, she will leave just like you did." That was such a sigh of relief. I am not worried about how my ex treats his new woman now, but fresh out of the marriage, I was asking that question. The fact that God just revealed this to me last year, lets me know that this is something that I needed to share with other women. After God reveals something to me my response is normally, "Oh, okay."

It makes a lot of sense. If we had someone of great importance to us, but we lost them we would treat a new person so much better if we ever got another opportunity to have a relationship. I know there are women who want to fight the new woman. It is not worth it ladies. Let her deal with the headache you just left. Focus on your well-being. That is most important. Let God handle him. He can whip him better than we can.

DATING AGAIN

When you are ready to start dating again, give it a try. Do not settle for anybody just because you want to say you are in a relationship. Get to know the person and what they enjoy. Let them know the things you enjoy. I will say, when I started dating again, I gave God a list of the things I wanted my next boyfriend to have: a driver's license, his own apartment, a car, a job, to be God-fearing, a good man, and no kids. I guess I instantly forgot I had a kid, so I revised my list and said, "Okay, he can have one." Believe it or not, I was meeting men that did not have a license and they were of age. I also asked, "Can he also be taller than me?" Hey, it was worth asking!

I went on several dates but only let one of them meet my daughter. I did not want her to meet them all. I did not want her around them, especially if I knew I was not ready to marry any of them. I did not want her around men that I did not know well enough to know I could trust them.

I started dating my soon-to-be-husband in 2004, and we were married in 2009. Ladies, he had the following: a driver's license, his own apartment, a car, a job, he is God-fearing, a good man, has no kids, and he is taller than me! Yes!! I am just saying: no prayers are too small or silly for God. Put your request in and if it is meant to be, he will fulfill the request. Smile, ladies, we are worth it!

GOING DOWN THE SAME ROAD

We know the signs now. We know the triggers. If you see those signs, be prepared to let go and move on. You do not need to go down that road again. It is too costly. If you are still carrying baggage from the abusive relationship, you need to drop it off at the nearest dump. I was carrying baggage, and I did not even know it. After an argument, my husband told me that I enjoyed arguing. Of course, I denied it. Why would I enjoy arguing? Not me! But when I got home that night, I thought about how I was acting and how quick I reacted.

I decided that I did enjoy arguing and he made me realize it. A lot of times we get used to doing something repeatedly, and we think that behavior is normal. Although I had left the abusive relationship, I was still carrying loads of baggage. I had to find a new normal. I had to learn how not to have a quick comeback jab whenever we had an argument.

Now we have arguments maybe four times a year. I can see how much I have grown in that area. Our arguments now are called disagreements. I look at his point of view instead of just sticking with mine, and that is it.

THERE ARE GOOD MEN OUT THERE

Ladies for the record, all men do not cheat. I am not saying they have never cheated, but there are good men in this world. While you are single, take time to love who you are. Do not let your past mistakes or bad decisions bog you down. If you have children, love on them, too. When we love ourselves, we can then love a man.

God will send you the right one. Do not assume every guy who smiles at you in passing is the right one. When you are on your first date, listen while he is speaking instead of thinking things like, "This may be him. He may be the one." This is only the first date. Calm down and take it slow. Everyone is nice on the first date, including you! Listen to what he says. Watch how he treats you.

Sometimes we are not happy with ourselves and go out and try to enhance things. If God wanted you to have what you thought you lacked, whether it is boobs, a butt, or whatever, then he would have given it to you. I know we can buy a new look nowadays, but what is on the inside? Even with all of that added, who are you? What do you want out of life? How do you feel about you? Will he still want you without the enhancements? Now that is the real question. A man who truly loves us will love us regardless of how we look, how we are shaped, our skin color, or how much money we have. If you end up marrying this person, what happens when your youth or health is gone? Will he wash your feet when you are unable to bend down to reach them? Ladies, let's think about the most important things first.

YOU HAVE WHAT YOU NEED

We have what we need ladies. For a long time, I complained about not having things. I felt I did not know my mom's father and his side of the family. I complained that I was not around my dad's father and his side of the family enough as a kid. But what God recently revealed to me was that I was around the right side of the family that I needed to be around.

God put me around strong women who could teach me about life even when I thought I was just hanging around them to be with other kids. They did not have much but they had what they needed. They had what I needed to make me the woman I am today. They were old-school and I loved it. These five sisters were grateful for what they had, and they knew how to make it spread. There were a lot of kids around and they could whip up a meal and make it stretch. These sisters showed me how to be respectful to myself and others. They showed me what family is supposed to look like by sticking together at all costs. These sisters helped build my foundation, and now I can give them their flowers while they yet live, something they taught me, too.

God showed me how their brothers were respectful men. How they loved their wives, kids, parents, God, and their church. God showed me that what I thought were hard-core mothers of the church, were just women teaching me how to be respectful in God's house. I did not like the discipline as a kid, but as an adult, I thank God for it all. We do not understand things as kids, but when we get older, if we make it, we can look back and have more respect for the teachers or people that we thought were getting on our nerves.

God showed me how he placed intelligent and respectful women in my life that I could watch during my teen and adult years, women that could show me how to carry myself as a lady and how to act as a woman. You never know who is watching you. Thanks, Dajuana T.

God showed me how the same choir songs that I complained about singing repeatedly as a kid, would be the same songs I sing when I am going through something in life. Those songs helped me make it through hard times.

God showed me how much I enjoyed church as a kid. I felt so much love when guest churches visited. Everyone was so happy. They hugged and kissed everyone. We seemed like a big happy church family.

One day I mentioned how I thought I got more hugs and kisses from the church than I did from my mom. God stopped me and said, "Your mom could only give you what she knew to give, and what she had to give, but what she did not give you, you got from the church and those five sisters." I then said, "Oh, okay." God has a way of revealing things to me when I am standing in front of my bathroom mirror. I am not complaining, because sometimes I call him, and he does not answer. It does not mean he is not there, I believe he wants me to make some decisions on my own without asking him everything. How do I know? He told me.

We can go through life being upset or holding grudges with family or friends, not realizing that they didn't have what we wanted from them, or they did not know how to give it to us. After God recently revealed this to me, I thought, "Wow, I had everything I needed this entire time! Now what I do with it is all up to me." He has me covered, even when I did not know it. If he has me, then he has you, too. I am no different than you. I was born and will die just like you. What I do in between is all up to me, just like it is all up to you.

MY PRAYER

I hope and pray this book has encouraged you to stay
strong. Life is not always easy, but it is possible, as one of
my favorite motivational speakers would say. Do not let
this world tear you down. Just remember, we all make
mistakes and will continue to make them. Do not be so hard
on yourself. If God wakes you up above ground tomorrow,
you can try again. Be strong and do not give up.

TAKE THE FIRST STEP
ASK FOR HELP

What I have learned in life is that we must take the first step. If I do not take that step of faith, I cannot get to the next step. Once you step out, it is amazing. It is scary at first, but you will eventually look back and say, "Why didn't I do this a long time ago?"

I am so glad I took that step of faith. Our daughter graduated from high school in 2016. God has also blessed me with a wonderful husband and another daughter. Life is good. God is good. He is showing me things for my future that I never knew were possible. I hold no grudges with my ex-husband. It took a while. I had to realize that focusing on what happened in my past took way too much of my energy and time. I cannot change any of it. I have to focus on my future. That was negative energy. I had to let it go and move on to better life experiences. It does get better. You just have to take the steps to get there. We cannot change what happened in our past, but we can change our future…Get Up and RUN.

Be respectful, meaning do not kill him. He will get his share for mistreating God's Princess, and you will get your blessings for being faithful. Just run and we can talk later.

Several resources available for you:

Domestic Violence Helpline	1-800-356-6767
Bridges Domestic Violence Center	1-615-599-5777
Center of Hope	1-931-381-8580
Families in Crisis, Inc.	1-800-675-0766
YWCA	1-800-334-4628